111
Ways to
Bounce Back

Kate —
Let's do amazing
things together &
make the world a
more beautiful place!

Love
Ina
xx
oo

Tasfil Publishing LLC
New Jersey, USA
www.tasfil.com

Editor's Note: In order to avoid awkward "he/she," "him/her" references, the plural "they" or "their" has often been used to refer to singular antecedents such as "person" or "partner' even though this construction doesn't adhere to strict grammatical rules.

Cover Design: Laura Jacoby

ISBN: 9781726616409

Other books by this author:

Life Happens: Bounce Back!
Divorce Happens: Bounce Back!

The beauty of life is that every day we are gifted with the opportunity to grow, evolve, and change to become the best possible version of ourselves. To take full advantage of those gifts, every morning I do what I call *create my day* to make sure that I have the inner strength to handle whatever I will be faced with.

I wake up two hours before I really need to so that I have the time to set my intentions for the day; to organize myself so that I manage my time, my thoughts and my energy; and to read through my list of the things I am so very grateful for. My morning time creates my day by helping me take responsibility for how I respond to my day, every day. It helps me achieve my ultimate goal of having my mind, body, and soul work as one, so that the best version of me greets the world each and every day.

Before learning to create my day, I would jump out of bed and go on autopilot. I would spend the remainder of the day impulsively reacting to whatever came at me. By the time I'd go to bed at night, I'd be exhausted and feeling stressed over what could have been done better or what didn't get done at all.

Intentionally creating my day is something that came out of the **Four-Step Plan to Bounce Back** that I wrote about in my book, *Life Happens: Bounce Back!* As I expressed in that book, after realizing it was my own insecurities that were keeping me from achieving the life I wanted, I went on a journey of self-discovery to find out where those insecurities came from.

In short, I learned I had built a belief system that said I wasn't good enough, smart enough, pretty enough, or whatever enough. That belief system, in turn, was built on the fact that I lacked self-love and self-appreciation. You see, if you don't love yourself, you can't develop the resiliency to bounce back from negative situations. Instead, you often find yourself in similar negative situations: the faces and events might change, but the situation is one that's all too familiar.

Because I was able to change my beliefs about myself, my life changed. Now I have the self-love to know that I am worthy of having the life of my dreams. Knowing that helps me overcome obstacles. Remembering that helps me bounce back from adversity. My Four-Step Plan is what I developed to help me find self-love. Now I use it to help me stop a negative cycle or to change something in my life. And I promise you, through self-love, you too, can have the life of your dreams.

In case you're interested, here's a summary of my Four-Step Plan. If you'd like to learn more, I encourage you to check out my book, *Life Happens: Bounce Back!* to get full details on how to complete each step.

The Four-step Bounce Back Into You plan.

Step 1: *Get Clarity.* Recognize the situations in your life that are making you unhappy and the underlying beliefs that helped create those situations.

Step 2: *Get Real.* Determine exactly what your responsibilities and roles are in your negative situations.

Step 3: *Get a Vision*. Figure out what the best version of you is, and what kind of life you really want to have.

Step 4: *Get Going!* Create a plan to change your beliefs so that you can create the life you want.

The emphasis in all the above steps is on how important it is to learn to love ourselves. There is one very important lesson that I live by: once you learn to love yourself and believe in yourself, the rest of your life will fall into place. I know I cannot bounce back from when life happens without loving myself unconditionally.

But bouncing back is ongoing. For me, the term means continually overcoming the curveballs that life throws our way, whether it's failed relationships, financial hardships, loss of loved ones, or just getting through a stressful day.

The key to bouncing back is knowing and believing that there is simply no one like you and that you deserve to be happy. We are born to be our unique selves; we are all perfectly imperfect. We—including you and me—are all good enough.

And now, it is with that sentiment, and great excitement and joy, that I share with you **111 Ways to Bounce Back into You** in the following pages.

My wish for you is that you take the time to embrace and try one of my tips every day. They will help you get to know who you are, remind you of life's journey, and help you fall in love with yourself—which means, they will help you bounce back from life's adversaries.

As you do them, remember: don't be hard on yourself. Have fun with these exercises, let them become a joyful part of your life.

After each tip, I invite you to reflect and write something directly on the page that the tip inspires you to write. Continue writing on separate paper if you desire to add more. I love to write and journal about my day-to-day life. It helps provide clarity on what I'm experiencing and helps me see just how far I have come. I'm sure you'll find similar benefits.

So, enjoy the tips and write something that speaks to you. Then tell me about it! You can contact me via my website, www.LisaBien.com. I would love to hear from you and learn how you are doing.

This thing called life is a journey for all of us. It is a very human experience so we need to remember to be kind to ourselves. But most importantly we need to remember that *every day* we have a chance to become the best version of ourselves.

Keep it going and become the best version of YOU!

111

Ways to
Bounce Back

Breathe.
Take a deep breath in. As you exhale, remind yourself **you've got this.** Take another deep breath and repeat. Your mind is listening and hears what you're saying. Your mind and body work together and react from your thoughts.
Fill your mind with good thoughts.
What other mantras can you say to remind you of how strong and capable you really are?

1

_____

_____

_____

_____

_____

_____

_____

_____

_____

_____

_____

_____

_____

_____

_____

2 Think about something you did in the past when you succeeded. *That* is evidence of your true self. Briefly describe that event and how it felt. Let it remind you that **you will get through this, too.**

_____

_____

_____

_____

_____

_____

_____

_____

_____

_____

_____

_____

_____

_____

_____

_____

Smile. It feels so good to smile. When we smile, **it makes our whole being feel good.** Write about someone who makes you smile, or about something. Why do you smile when you think about the person or thing?

3

_____

_____

_____

_____

_____

_____

_____

_____

_____

_____

_____

_____

_____

_____

_____

4 Step outside in the sunshine. **Feel the warmth.** It's good for your soul. I believe the sun is our reminder from God, the Universe, or however you wish to refer to a Supreme Being, that you are **love**. Write about love...what it looks like and how it feels to you.

_____

_____

_____

_____

_____

_____

_____

_____

_____

_____

_____

_____

_____

_____

_____

_____

_____

_____

Get **quiet** with yourself. **Hug** yourself. Yes! Go ahead and hug yourself, feel the love from yourself. **All the love you need is right inside of your soul.** After you hug yourself, write about how special you are and what makes you, *you*.

5

_____

_____

_____

_____

_____

_____

_____

_____

_____

_____

_____

_____

_____

_____

_____

_____

_____

_____

6 Take your right hand and place it above your heart. **Feel your heart beat.** Pay attention to what makes it speed up or slow down. Practice paying attention to your body and what makes your heart feel good. **Feeling your heart can help you begin to listen to what your body is telling you about an experience or a person.** Write about what you are feeling right now. If you are questioning a relationship in your life, think on it while you feel your heartbeat, then write about how you feel when you spend time with that person.

_____

_____

_____

_____

_____

_____

_____

_____

_____

_____

_____

_____

_____

_____

_____

Exercise. Do not make it harder than it has to be. I used to do that. I would make excuses that it was too hard to exercise. I needed new sneakers. I didn't belong to a gym. Whatever reason I could think of to skip it, I'd find it. Do not skip it. **Just get up and walk.** Wear the old sneakers and walk outside. Think about how exercise makes you feel, or the difference it would make in your life. Then complete this thought: if I started to exercise today, and made a commitment to continue doing it, it would make me.

7

_____

_____

_____

_____

_____

_____

_____

_____

_____

_____

_____

_____

_____

8 Put your phone down. Do it now or schedule a date to go phone-free. **Challenge yourself.** Try not to look at your phone for one hour a day. Start there and then add additional time as you begin to see how nice it can be to disconnect from your phone. **We all need quiet time.** Now, write about how it feels to go phone-free.

_____

_____

_____

_____

_____

_____

_____

_____

_____

_____

_____

_____

_____

_____

_____

_____

_____

Take a social media break. We all need this. Social media is the highlighted reel from someone else's life. It's okay to engage in it, but it's also okay to take a necessary break – preferably daily. Try to take a full day off, or as long as you can go, and write about how the experience felt.

9

_____

_____

_____

_____

_____

_____

_____

_____

_____

_____

_____

_____

_____

_____

_____

_____

_____

10

Clean out your drawers. Start with just one. Pick one and declutter it. **It is essential to clean out the clutter from your physical space.** Do you feel accomplished? How do you feel?

_____

_____

_____

_____

_____

_____

_____

_____

_____

_____

_____

_____

_____

_____

_____

_____

Clean your house. Pick a room that you have been avoiding, and do it. It always makes me feel accomplished when I clean out the clutter. Start with baby steps if you want to and **commit to just 15 minutes a day** to get rid of whatever you can. To help you stay motivated, think about how good it will feel when you are done. Describe that feeling here:

11

_____

_____

_____

_____

_____

_____

_____

_____

_____

_____

_____

_____

_____

_____

_____

_____

12

Get organized. Go through files. Sort out and donate old clothes. Organization is not underrated. Again, just **commit to 15 minutes** at a time if that's all you have right now. What physical spaces or areas of your life do you think could be better organized? How do you think you'll feel when you have them the way you want them to be?

_____

_____

_____

_____

_____

_____

_____

_____

_____

_____

_____

_____

_____

_____

_____

Buy flowers for yourself. What is **your favorite flower?** Go out and buy it for you. Smell it. Look at it. Remember: **You are as beautiful as that flower.** Describe the flowers then think on and write about what it means to give yourself something so beautiful.

13

14

Call someone you love and tell them how you feel. It feels good when we remember to make that call and say, "**I love you!**" Now, how did the call go?

_____

_____

_____

_____

_____

_____

_____

_____

_____

_____

_____

_____

_____

_____

_____

_____

Sometimes you need to push yourself. You tell yourself that you're tired, or don't have time, or whatever as an excuse. But maybe if you pushed yourself you could do something that you have been meaning to do – whatever it is. Bake a cake. Call a friend. **Push through it.** Now write about how good it feels to have accomplished whatever you just pushed through.

15

_____

_____

_____

_____

_____

_____

_____

_____

_____

_____

_____

_____

_____

_____

_____

_____

16

Rejection is okay. It does not mean you are not worthy. Acknowledge that the **rejection means that experience wasn't right for you in the first place.** Write about a time when you felt rejected but **learned or benefited by the outcome** (e.g., when a job or a relationship didn't work out).

_____

_____

_____

_____

_____

_____

_____

_____

_____

_____

_____

_____

_____

_____

_____

_____

_____

You are worth it. Believe it. Tell yourself that,
until you believe it. Write it down!

17

_____

_____

_____

_____

_____

_____

_____

_____

_____

_____

_____

_____

_____

_____

_____

18

Write down the **5 things that make you, YOU.**
What's unique about you? Come on!
You can do it.

_____

_____

_____

_____

_____

_____

_____

_____

_____

_____

_____

_____

_____

_____

_____

_____

_____

Remember **you are loved.** Remind yourself as much as you need to. Write a love letter to yourself. Tell yourself what **you love about being you the most.** Bookmark this page and continue to refer to it.

19

20

Enjoy your favorite warm beverage. Sit down and have some of your favorite tea, coffee, or other drink with the intention of focusing on it and enjoying it. **Get present** with the act of drinking it Write about the experience – did you notice anything different about the drink? Do you feel differently after you drank it?

_____

_____

_____

_____

_____

_____

_____

_____

_____

_____

_____

_____

_____

_____

Watch your favorite movie and do not forget the
popcorn! Now, why is it your favorite?

21

_____

_____

_____

_____

_____

_____

_____

_____

_____

_____

_____

_____

_____

_____

_____

_____

_____

_____

22

Make a date-night – with yourself. Take yourself out anywhere you want to go. **Where did you go?** What did you enjoy?

_____

_____

_____

_____

_____

_____

_____

_____

_____

_____

_____

_____

_____

_____

_____

_____

_____

Write **something nice** to yourself on at least 10 Post-it notes. Put them around the house where you will see them. Make the list here, first.

23

24

Ask yourself if you are being judgmental regarding yourself or another person. **Being non-judgmental is an important tool for bouncing back** from a negative situation because it saves you from getting stuck in negativity. For example, let's say you just went through a bad break-up and discover your ex posted something untrue about you on social media. Being angry is a perfectly natural response. But if you go beyond anger and make a judgment call, you may think something like: "He is such a liar! He's just an awful person!" you risk getting stuck in anger and feeling like a victim. On the other hand, if you stick to the facts and what you can control (you), you may express surprise over his post and see it for what it is: his way of trying to handle the breakup. Since his ways have nothing to do with you, the anger will lift, and you won't feel victimized. The art of being non-judgmental is hard. The first step comes in recognizing when you are being judgmental. Can you think of any areas in your life where you might need to re-evaluate whether you're being judgmental?

_____

_____

_____

_____

_____

_____

_____

_____

Put your slippers on and walk around the house with no purpose or aim. Just **feel the comfort**. What else can you do to be comfortable—what works for you? Make a list of things here that you can do to feel comfortable and refer to it whenever you're stressed and need help finding ease.

25

26

Choose a healthy food to eat because **you** want **to be healthy**. Not because someone else tells you to. You have to want to do this for yourself. What kinds of healthy foods do you like to eat? How do you feel about yourself when you make healthy choices?

_____

_____

_____

_____

_____

_____

_____

_____

_____

_____

_____

_____

_____

_____

_____

Light a candle with the intention to allow the
glow of the flame and the scent of it to help
you decompress and **take time to reflect on your
day.** What could you do better? Did you over
react to someone? Think about the why: why
did you overreact what was the real reason behind it? Write it
down and journal about how you can change that behavior for
next time. Maybe it's *I won't overreact when my friend cancels
plans* or *I will work on begin more understanding.*

27

28

Wear your favorite perfume. Breathe it in and **delight** in the pretty smell. What does the smell make you think of? Why do you like it?

_____

_____

_____

_____

_____

_____

_____

_____

_____

_____

_____

_____

_____

_____

_____

Recognize your **success**. If you did something today such as starting a new eating plan, acknowledge it. And I mean *really* acknowledge it. Write it down and include how **awesome you are** and you feel about the success. Refer to this anytime you need a little boost of encouragement.

29

_____

_____

_____

_____

_____

_____

_____

_____

_____

_____

_____

_____

_____

_____

_____

_____

30

Do not forget to **laugh**. Sometimes you just have to laugh. Laughter reminds us not to take ourselves too seriously. Think about the last time you had a really good belly laugh. If you cannot remember, then call the funniest person you know, or turn on your favorite comedy and laugh. Write down how you felt and before the laugh and how laughing made you feel. Did it help?

_____

_____

_____

_____

_____

_____

_____

_____

_____

_____

_____

_____

_____

_____

Committing to **self-care is key**. It can be one simple thing that is in your mind and you keep saying "I need to do this." Write down what you can commit to doing to take good care of yourself. Then do it!

31

_____

_____

_____

_____

_____

_____

_____

_____

_____

_____

_____

_____

_____

_____

_____

_____

_____

32

Be kind to yourself. I like to remind people not to say anything to themselves that they would not say to their own best friend. Do not beat yourself up and begin to think everything in your life awful. People often do that—when one negative thing happen, they'll remind themselves of all the other negative things, building momentum until they're just miserable. Nothing good comes from that. Instead, whatever happens, remember to **be kind to yourself**. Remind yourself what you did right. What kinds of good things that you've said or done can you remind yourself about?

_____

_____

_____

_____

_____

_____

_____

_____

_____

_____

_____

_____

_____

_____

Do not let a situation define who you are. Part of being able to love yourself is to be really, really **self-aware**. If you are going through a tough time, remember that is not who you are, it's just an experience. Write about who you are today and what you are doing to make your situation better. For example, if you are going through a divorce and feel like a failure, remember that you are not a failure and "going through a divorce" is not the definition of who you are. But instead, you are someone taking care of yourself. You are someone looking out for your best interests. You are_____

33

_____

_____

_____

_____

_____

_____

_____

_____

_____

_____

_____

_____

_____

_____

_____

_____

34

You have **the power to change** your life whenever you want. Write down your goals. Look at them every day and remind yourself that you, and only you, can change the direction of your life.

Seek support. There is such a **great feeling** that comes with knowing that you have a friend or two that will always support you. Seek it if you need it and when you need it. Friends have a way of helping us along during adversity.

35

Journal about what you are going through and ask yourself how can my friend help?

_____

_____

_____

_____

_____

_____

_____

_____

_____

_____

_____

_____

_____

_____

_____

_____

_____

36

Look forward. Write down what you want your life to look like in 3 months, 6 months and 9 months. Then, close your eyes every night before you go to bed and **picture what your life will look like in the future.** If you can think it, it can happen for you.

_____

_____

_____

_____

_____

_____

_____

_____

_____

_____

_____

_____

_____

_____

_____

Honesty is key to personal growth and learning. **Be honest with yourself.** I mean really honest, and look for ways you could have handled a situation better or smarter. What did you learn about it or about yourself that will come in handy in the future? This is a healthy exercise to get to know yourself.

37

_____

_____

_____

_____

_____

_____

_____

_____

_____

_____

_____

_____

_____

_____

_____

_____

_____

_____

38 Patience. Stop looking for life's answers to come quickly or from someone else. **Be patient with yourself** and eventually you will realize that you have all the answers, you always had them, and they will reveal themselves when they are supposed to. Where do you need to find patience in your life and learn to trust yourself more?

_____

_____

_____

_____

_____

_____

_____

_____

_____

_____

_____

_____

_____

_____

_____

_____

_____

Look around and see who is in your life. Think about **someone who supports you**, who always makes you laugh, or is always there with a hot cup of coffee. Make a list of people you love and who love you.

39

_____

_____

_____

_____

_____

_____

_____

_____

_____

_____

_____

_____

_____

_____

_____

_____

_____

40 Surround yourself with reminders of what
makes you special. For example, take old notes
or birthday cards and hang them where you can
see them to remind you of how special you are.
Write out what those reminders say.

_____

_____

_____

_____

_____

_____

_____

_____

_____

_____

_____

_____

_____

_____

_____

During some of my toughest times, (e.g., financial bankruptcy, starting my own business, and going through my second divorce all at once) I forced myself to **begin the day with a smile**. For me, when I smile it makes me feel good inside. Write three things that make you smile and sit there and smile as your write them. A smile can help you feel better from the outside in.

41

_____

_____

_____

_____

_____

_____

_____

_____

_____

_____

_____

_____

_____

_____

_____

42

Take a walk outside. Being around nature can make you **feel better**. Write down how being outdoors makes you feel. Write about where you like to be and why? Write a pledge to yourself to spend more time where you like being.

_____

_____

_____

_____

_____

_____

_____

_____

_____

_____

_____

_____

_____

_____

_____

_____

Open yourself up to **forgiveness**. When you hold
on to hurt and pain, it only continues to harm
you. Whom do you need to forgive? How will it
feel for you to forgive them?

43

_____

_____

_____

_____

_____

_____

_____

_____

_____

_____

_____

_____

_____

_____

_____

_____

_____

44 Growing up I believed that life was supposed to be easy. I have no idea where that came from. Perhaps from watching TV and romanticizing life. Well, now I know that life is not easy, it comes with lots of ups and downs, and that we have very little control over what happens to us. What **we can control is our expectations and reactions to life**. When I was in the midst of some really challenging times, I never lost hope that life would get better. It is important to have **faith** that things will get better. Journal about a time in your life where hope got you through and ask yourself is this another possible time?

_____

_____

_____

_____

_____

_____

_____

_____

_____

_____

_____

_____

_____

Become a better communicator.

Communication is key. Do a short survey of the people you love and trust, and ask them a question or two about your communication skills. List their names and answers here. Find out from them what you need to work on.

45

_____

_____

_____

_____

_____

_____

_____

_____

_____

_____

_____

_____

_____

_____

_____

_____

_____

_____

46

Hang out with **quality people**. Who brings you up? Write their names here and mention why or how they positively influence you. Call, reach out, read an old email from that person, or somehow find a way to **connect** with that person.

_____

_____

_____

_____

_____

_____

_____

_____

_____

_____

_____

_____

_____

_____

_____

Have the **right mindset**. Getting through
adversity requires a change in your belief about
the challenges. If you are going through
bankruptcy and you walk around saying "I will
never get out of this negative situation" or ""I
am a loser because I allowed this to happen," then you will
remain stuck in this negative mindset. **Your thoughts are key**. Be
very mindful of what you are thinking about all day. For one day,
write down the theme to most of your thoughts. Remember, it is
not what happens to you in life, it is important to remember it is
how you respond to it.

47

_____

_____

_____

_____

_____

_____

_____

_____

_____

_____

_____

_____

_____

_____

48 Remind yourself that **you are loved**. Create an I LOVE YOU board or box and put cards, notes, handmade ornaments, or anything else on it to make it your special box. The goal is that it reminds you that you are loved and have love in your life. Write and/or plan what you think your love board should include. I like having reminders in my home and my office about the people I love and who love me.

_____

_____

_____

_____

_____

_____

_____

_____

_____

_____

_____

_____

_____

_____

_____

_____

Although change can happen in an instant, adapting to it takes time. In seconds, husbands can surprise you with a divorce announcement, or a doctor's visit can turn disastrous. When change happens, be patient with yourself as you learn to deal with it and bounce back. Journal about what changes you are going through and why it's only natural that it takes time to get through it.

49

_____

_____

_____

_____

_____

_____

_____

_____

_____

_____

_____

_____

_____

_____

_____

_____

50

You have to **believe in yourself**. Create a personal mantra that uses the word "believe" in it. Write out several below and practice saying them to yourself every day. For example, "I believe that I will become a motivational speaker and touch people's lives."

_____

_____

_____

_____

_____

_____

_____

_____

_____

_____

_____

_____

_____

_____

_____

_____

_____

Celebrate your successes list! Write down a
recent success and refer to it to remind and
energize you and remember to add to the list of
success as you reach your goals.

51

_____

_____

_____

_____

_____

_____

_____

_____

_____

_____

_____

_____

_____

_____

_____

_____

_____

_____

52

Drink water. Keeping your body hydrated is so important. **Your body and mind need water.** Write about how you take care of your body.

Make sleep a priority. Make sure you are sleeping at least 8 hours a day. When you are faced with adversity, your body and mind need rest, so you can be fresh the next day to face the situation. What can you change in your evening routine to help encourage you to get a good night's rest?

53

_____

_____

_____

_____

_____

_____

_____

_____

_____

_____

_____

_____

_____

_____

_____

_____

_____

_____

54

Take personal responsibility and evaluate a role you participated in that wasn't the best for you. **Be honest** about your decisions. Write about the situation and about what you could have done to make it better.

_____

_____

_____

_____

_____

_____

_____

_____

_____

_____

_____

_____

_____

_____

_____

_____

_____

Remind yourself every day that **you deserve to live the life you want,** not the life that someone else wants you to live. Write that affirmation down: *I deserve to live the life I want.* And then fill the page with affirmations to back it up. *I am worthy of a good life. I am a good person.*

55

_____

_____

_____

_____

_____

_____

_____

_____

_____

_____

_____

_____

_____

_____

_____

_____

_____

_____

56

Change constantly happens every day. Write about a recent change that happened in your life. Now, be present and mindful for a minute, take time to decide if the change is positive or negative. Then **make a plan** for dealing with the change.

_____

_____

_____

_____

_____

_____

_____

_____

_____

_____

_____

_____

_____

_____

_____

_____

_____

_____

Challenge yourself. Write down the areas of
your life where you want to grow and how you
intend to start making positive changes there.
For example, maybe you want to become a
better communicator with your children. Write it
down with specifies. *(Your name) will work on growing and
learning how to communicate with (X) on a daily basis. First, I will
repeat to myself what they said. Second, I will look at the
communication from their perspective. Third, I will speak to (X) in
a loving manner to ensure that my thoughts are communicated
clearly and concise.*

57

58 When I was going through my second divorce, I was very realistic in what my new life would look like. **Realistic self-reflection** was important. I knew my life would be different and that that did not mean it would be worse or terrible or anything like that. I knew it would just be different. Think about your life today and the challenges you are facing. Write a realistic summary of your what's going on and how you can use it as an opportunity for a change or easy solution.

_____

_____

_____

_____

_____

_____

_____

_____

_____

_____

_____

_____

_____

_____

Begin your day with a **Morning Moment of Appreciation**. Before you get out of bed, remind yourself about the beauty in your life. Write a list of things you appreciate and use this list to help you do your Morning Moment of Appreciation.

59

_____

_____

_____

_____

_____

_____

_____

_____

_____

_____

_____

_____

_____

_____

_____

_____

_____

_____

_____

60

Do not be afraid to make mistakes. We all do. The important thing is to remember to **learn** from them. What have you learned from mistakes you've made that makes your life better now?

_____

_____

_____

_____

_____

_____

_____

_____

_____

_____

_____

_____

_____

_____

_____

Make today the day you **take action** – whatever
it is. Maybe you have been saying *I should go*
to the gym first thing in the morning and you
haven't gone yet. Make today the day you
change your thought process and say *I will go*
to gym and find a convenient time that fits in my schedule and
then go! Write about the difference of saying *I should* vs. *I will*
go to the gym, whatever it is you have been putting off.

61

_____

_____

_____

_____

_____

_____

_____

_____

_____

_____

_____

_____

_____

_____

_____

62

Once you learn more about who you are and what you want, **remind yourself not to settle** for anything less than what you truly want and desire. I was the girl who would settle in certain relationships for less than what I really wanted. As I developed greater self-esteem, I realized I did not have to settle for less-than. What do you really want your life to look like? Are genuinely happy with your decisions? If not, write why you are not happy – did you settle?

_____

_____

_____

_____

_____

_____

_____

_____

_____

_____

_____

_____

_____

_____

_____

_____

Protect what you allow in your mind. **Watch what you say to yourself every day.** Watch your thoughts and when you hear something negative, stop it and work to think something positive. What are frequent negative habitual thoughts that you think about yourself now? Write them down now so you can become more aware of the next time they start to pop into your mind. Also try to come up with alternative thoughts to replace them.

63

64 I had to learn to stop being a people pleaser. Life is not a popularity contest. I still have to remind myself on occasion that not everyone will agree with me and that's okay. **We are all different.** Write about a time you did not agree with someone, or didn't really want to do something, and you did it anyway. Why did you capitulate? How could you have handled that situation differently?

_____

_____

_____

_____

_____

_____

_____

_____

_____

_____

_____

_____

_____

_____

_____

Decide what you want your life to look like.
What **small changes** can you start to implement
over the next day, then week, then month that
will propel you toward getting your life to look
like that?

65

---

66 Write down your **hopes** and refer to them as needed. I remember going through a tough time and I wore a bracelet that said *hope*. It was a reminder to me that there is always hope.

_____

_____

_____

_____

_____

_____

_____

_____

_____

_____

_____

_____

_____

_____

_____

_____

_____

_____

Create a **Vision Board**. If you can see it, you can
make it happen. Hang the board in a place
where you will see it every day, preferably,
multiple times a day. Diagram your vision board
here: what areas of your life do you want to
focus on? What images reflect those areas and your goals?

67

_____

_____

_____

_____

_____

_____

_____

_____

_____

_____

_____

_____

_____

_____

_____

68 **Let it go**. Let go of what you are holding onto inside. When we let go, we release the toxins from our mind, body and soul. I write down my inner thoughts, read them, and then I visualize me releasing the negative thoughts and emotions. I remind myself that I **want to grow** and let go of the stuff that is not working for me anymore. Being aware of thoughts that are not working for you is a big step in learning to love who you are. When we love ourselves, we know who we are, and we protect our mind, body and soul.

_____

_____

_____

_____

_____

_____

_____

_____

_____

_____

_____

_____

_____

_____

Manage your time. Take time to manage your time and think about the steps that you need to take to create time just for you. Write down what a day in your life looks like and then where can you add time in your schedule just for you. I always find that writing something down and seeing it on paper makes me really digest the information.

69

70

Map out your life. I love to take big sheets of poster board and map out my life: *Here is where I am today and here is what my next move is.* When we see where we are and where we want to go, it helps us **visualize** our road ahead. Sometimes I will say "why bother?" but then I review my old poster boards and I realize I am following the road map I created.

_____

_____

_____

_____

_____

_____

_____

_____

_____

_____

_____

_____

_____

_____

_____

_____

_____

Meditate. Download an app to walk you through the steps. It takes time and patience. Once you start, you won't want to stop. Journal about what you are mediating about. Maybe keep a **Mediation log** and see if you can find a theme to what you are mediating about the most.

71

_____

_____

_____

_____

_____

_____

_____

_____

_____

_____

_____

_____

_____

_____

_____

_____

_____

72

Remind yourself: **you can grow** from this. Challenge yourself to find a way to do it. Can you make a list of good things that have come from similar situations? Can you come up with a list of good things that could come from this one?

_____

_____

_____

_____

_____

_____

_____

_____

_____

_____

_____

_____

_____

_____

_____

_____

_____

Fill your mind with **positive thoughts** and don't let the negative ones stay for very long. This is not so easy. Here is what I do. First, I know and recognize that there are constant thoughts in my head, all day long. When I hear a negative one or one that I makes me question it, I ask: "What was that thought?" I literally stop and have an internal dialogue to quiet my negative voice. I even tell the negative voice to be quiet. Try to recognize and change your internal dialogue and begin to journal what the ongoing thoughts are.

73

74

Remember **it is worth it**. If I had a dollar for each time I said to myself, "why I am going through this?" I could buy Manhattan. I once stayed in a relationship longer than I ever should have because I just didn't want to **make the change**. But it's never healthy to stay in any relationship that is not working for you. So remember, it is worth making the change. Journal your reasons why you want to make the change, and do not lose sight of your why!

_____

_____

_____

_____

_____

_____

_____

_____

_____

_____

_____

_____

_____

_____

Create Your Team! Sometimes during our toughest times we need to remember that we have a **team of people that will support us**. Stop and think about the people in your life that can help and or support you in one way or another. It does not have to be a friend or family member, sometimes it's a professor, colleague, your medical doctor. Write a list of people on your team to support you when you need it most.

75

_____

_____

_____

_____

_____

_____

_____

_____

_____

_____

_____

_____

_____

_____

76 Get up every day and get dressed. I have a friend that every time I see her, she is always dressed and looks **ready to conquer the day**. I once asked her about it and she said that when she is dressed, she feels better and more confident. So, I am going to share this, when I wear sweatpants and lounge around day after day, it makes me feel unproductive and down. I know myself so well, I know what works for me. I wake up and get dressed! Journal about how you feel and your motivation levels that come with your appearance.

_____

_____

_____

_____

_____

_____

_____

_____

_____

_____

_____

_____

_____

_____

Seek the positive. Find positive people. Spend time with people who make you feel good. Who makes you feel good? Journal about the last time you felt really really positive. What about that situation made you feel good?

77

_____

_____

_____

_____

_____

_____

_____

_____

_____

_____

_____

_____

_____

_____

_____

_____

78

Take up a new hobby. What have you always wanted to learn to do? **What can you do now** to help get you started?

_____

_____

_____

_____

_____

_____

_____

_____

_____

_____

_____

_____

_____

_____

_____

_____

I never believed I was smart enough until one day a college professor tapped me on the shoulder and told me I was. So, look at what you are putting in front of the sentence "I am not X enough." What **evidence** do you have to support this? Maybe it is time you revisit that statement. We all add something before the "enough." Watch what you put there. Journal about what you are saying about not being something enough.

79

_____

_____

_____

_____

_____

_____

_____

_____

_____

_____

_____

_____

_____

_____

_____

80

Learn to **trust yourself**. Your thoughts and your feelings are there for a reason. They are **your guide**. Think about something that happened in the past where your intuition was right on target. Write about that experience and express appreciation for being able to trust your gut feelings.

_____

_____

_____

_____

_____

_____

_____

_____

_____

_____

_____

_____

_____

_____

_____

_____

No one ever said that life would be easy and free of problems. But sometimes, we make it harder than it needs to be. **Ask** yourself, "Am I making this harder than it needs to be?" Then ask, **"how can I make it easier?"**

81

82

Get a mentor. I have been divorced twice. I have written a book on divorce, so I like to support people going through a divorce. **There are people who like to mentor people** going through a similar experience that can help you. Ask around and find a mentor to ask questions or just to listen. What areas in your life do you think would benefit from having a mentor? Whom could you approach about being one? Could you be a mentor for someone else? In what aspect?

_____

_____

_____

_____

_____

_____

_____

_____

_____

_____

_____

_____

_____

_____

To bounce back we need to **rebuild** and remind ourselves that it is always possible. Take it one moment at a time. **Moment, by moment**. Write out how far you've come already.

83

_____

_____

_____

_____

_____

_____

_____

_____

_____

_____

_____

_____

_____

_____

_____

_____

84

Do not quit on yourself. Keep moving forward. **Never stop working on your goals**. Take a look at your goals that you wrote before. Where are you in the process? It's not about how fast you move towards your personal goals, it's about how simply moving in the right direction that works for you. Evaluate, are you moving in the right direction?

_____

_____

_____

_____

_____

_____

_____

_____

_____

_____

_____

_____

_____

_____

_____

_____

_____

_____

Money will come and money will go. **Value the things you cannot put a price tag on.** Love, honesty, kindness, respect. Make a list of more things you value most.

85

_____

_____

_____

_____

_____

_____

_____

_____

_____

_____

_____

_____

_____

_____

_____

_____

_____

86

Do not take the **love** you have in your life for granted. **Value** it. **Treasure** it. Whom do you love? Who loves you? List them all and express your appreciation for them.

Be true to yourself, and do not compromise on what you really want from a relationship. Do not settle for less. Whether it's a boss, co-worker, friend, lover, or relative, ask yourself **what do you really want from your relationship** with that person? What do you want to give to it? What do you want to receive? How do you want that relationship to look?

87

88

Stop pining over what was, or could have been but wasn't, or should have been, or...just stop. Instead, **celebrate what is**. Most important, celebrate what will be! Journal about what YOU really want from the outcome of this situation.

Keep the **focus on you**. It's necessary, and not self-centered to focus on you, your thoughts, and your life plan. You get to direct your life. You are starring in your own movie of life. Whenever I am faced with any adversity in my life, I look inward to maintain my balance. Write down what you need to make you happy. Perhaps it's a yoga class, or mediation in the morning. Write what you need to get you through the day.

89

90 Create a balance plan. Take stock of what seems to be off kilter in your life and answer the following questions: What is bothering you the most? What can you do to fix it? What kind of plan can you make to put the situation into balance? **You will take the action** when you are ready. Sometimes just having the plan is enough.

_____

_____

_____

_____

_____

_____

_____

_____

_____

_____

_____

_____

_____

_____

_____

_____

Try to avoid situations that you know do not make you feel good. Identify the people who you must deal with, for example a co-worker, relative, or landlord, to name a few examples and make boundary plans. If you have a co-worker whom you clash with during certain situations, **prepare** for that situation. We cannot always avoid the people in our lives, but we can **create and strive to live with healthy boundaries**. With whom do you need boundaries? What can you do to prepare to interact with them?

91

_____

_____

_____

_____

_____

_____

_____

_____

_____

_____

_____

_____

_____

_____

_____

92

Be honest with yourself about the amount of effort you are putting into you, your work, and your family. **Make an effort log** on this page of the areas you want to see improvement in your life. Then ask yourself if you are giving 100 percent of your effort toward each one. If you're not, identify which areas you need to improve you focus.

_____

_____

_____

_____

_____

_____

_____

_____

_____

_____

_____

_____

_____

_____

_____

_____

_____

_____

Happiness is an inside job. We do not just wake
up happy. We have to create our happiness and
know what makes us happy. Write down the top
5 things that support your happiness. For
example, I know spending time with my
children makes me happy. I enjoy watching sports with them. A
hot shower with lavender soap makes me happy. Identify what
makes you happy? Make a happy journal. Carry it with you, \and
look at it as much as you need to.

93

_____

_____

_____

_____

_____

_____

_____

_____

_____

_____

_____

_____

_____

_____

94 Do not obsess about a negative interaction. Write down what happened to acknowledge that it happened. Now, look at the situation and ask what could you have done **better**? What was your role from the interaction? Learn from it and try to **move on**. I say try, because I know how sometimes we get thoughts stuck in our head and this is not an easy tip at all. But remember, it's in your head and that you control what goes on in there. Would you allow someone to twist your arm all day? No. So don't let them in your mind and twisting your emotion all day either.

_____

_____

_____

_____

_____

_____

_____

_____

_____

_____

_____

_____

_____

Get **comfortable with being alone**. Not always so easy. Journal about the experience of being alone. What did you do? What did you learn about yourself? I had to teach myself how to be alone. If you did not enjoy the alone time write about what you can do the next time you are alone to make it a better experience. For example, I would make sure I had a good book in the house at all times for my alone time.

95

96

Make a **plan for tomorrow**. What one thing can you do tomorrow that will help you bounce back or remind you of how special life is?

_____

_____

_____

_____

_____

_____

_____

_____

_____

_____

_____

_____

_____

_____

_____

_____

Eat a piece of chocolate or **deliberately indulge** (just a little) in a special treat you rarely let yourself do. Focus on the sweetness of the moment and record how good it feels to relish in the sweetness of life.

97

_____

_____

_____

_____

_____

_____

_____

_____

_____

_____

_____

_____

_____

_____

_____

_____

_____

_____

98

Laugh. Look for a quote, cartoon, or something else that will make you laugh. Write it down here to always remember it.

Focus on something else. When I am really sad or down about something in my life, I purposefully focus on something else. I will read or listen to motivational videos, or really just do anything to put my attention on something other than what I am going through. It is not healthy for anyone to sit and think about their divorce or money struggles all the time. **Deliberately change your focus** onto something positive, then write about the experience and how it felt to focus on something else.

99

100

Be true to yourself and do what you want to do. If you want to pass on attending an event then say "no." **Practice taking care of yourself** and listening to what you truly want to do. Ask yourself now if you are following through on that advice. Journal your questions and answers. Then ask where you need to say "no" more often.

_____

_____

_____

_____

_____

_____

_____

_____

_____

_____

_____

_____

_____

_____

_____

_____

Read, read and read. **Make a commitment to read** one book a month to help you learn more about the world. There are a lot of wonderful authors with lots of great ideas. Take time to become a student of yourself. Take a moment to browse a bookstore or ask friends for recommendations of good books. Write them down here so you always have a handy reference of books to get.

101

_____

_____

_____

_____

_____

_____

_____

_____

_____

_____

_____

_____

_____

_____

_____

_____

_____

102

Volunteerism is always good for my soul. When I **give back** to the community, knowing that I made an impact helps give me a sense of peace and accomplishment. Get out there and volunteer in your community and journal about the experience. Or journal about how you would like to give back. What can you offer others? Where can you find them to help them?

_____

_____

_____

_____

_____

_____

_____

_____

_____

_____

_____

_____

_____

_____

_____

Create your **Happy List**! Make a list of the things that make you happy and call it my go to Happy List. Once you have that list of hobbies or activities that you enjoy you can refer to this list when you are alone, find yourself feeling lonely, or just bored.

103

_____

_____

_____

_____

_____

_____

_____

_____

_____

_____

_____

_____

_____

_____

_____

_____

104

Remind yourself daily how far you have come. **Take a moment to reflect** on where you were at the beginning of this problem and compare it to where you are now. Make a list and elaborate on whatever success or piece of learning you've gained.

Create the **best-case scenario** for the situation. I like to write options for my outcomes, including several positive "what if..." questions. I write them all down. Then I review them and think about them. Often my best solutions come from this exercise.

105

106

Talk to the younger version of you. **Love** that innocent person. Let your young you know everything is okay. You might have felt unlovable, but you are loved and worth it today. Write an encouraging note to your younger self.

_____

_____

_____

_____

_____

_____

_____

_____

_____

_____

_____

_____

_____

_____

_____

_____

Learn how to **be honest** with yourself and everyone else. Sometimes the hardest thing to do is to be honest with ourselves. Write down whatever it is you are going through and try, try to look for opportunities to learn from it.

107

_____

_____

_____

_____

_____

_____

_____

_____

_____

_____

_____

_____

_____

_____

_____

_____

_____

108

Commit to yourself and what you need to do. For example, if you are unhappy at your job and you keep saying you need a new job, make a commitment to making that happen. Write your own personal commitment statement. Write it out here, then write it on many notes to place around your home to remind yourself of your commitment.

_____

_____

_____

_____

_____

_____

_____

_____

_____

_____

_____

_____

_____

_____

_____

_____

Honor and acknowledge your past. Without your past you would not be who you are today. Write a letter to your past. Thank your past for all that it taught you. The past is just that, the past. Now, let it go.

109

110

Hold your **head up high**. When I declared personal bankruptcy, I was so embarrassed that I did not tell anyone. Until I realized that it was simply a situation I found myself in and it was not who I was. It did not define me. Once I started telling people about it, I started to feel the emotional weight lift off my shoulders. I felt **relief**. Journal about your situation and if anyone knows. How do you think you would feel to share what you are going through?

_____

_____

_____

_____

_____

_____

_____

_____

_____

_____

_____

_____

_____

_____

_____

Treat yourself like your own best friend. If you don't, no one else will. Write a commitment to yourself about how you will treat yourself with love, kindness and respect.

111

_____

_____

_____

_____

_____

_____

_____

_____

_____

_____

_____

_____

_____

_____

_____

_____

About Lisa Bien

Speaker, TV host, and author Lisa Bien knows first-hand finding success in any area of life requires dedication, focus, self-confidence and resilience. With her trademark high energy and passion for storytelling she's a keynote speaker, workshop facilitator, and one-on-one coach for business professionals.

One of Lisa's strongest assets is her ability to combine humor and raw honesty to connect with her audience. In both of her books, *Life Happens: Bounce Back!* and *Divorce Happens: Bounce Back!*, she shares numerous autobiographical accounts of key events in her life that led to the creation of her *Bouncing Back* campaign.

Lisa is also the host of **BOUNCING BACK with Lisa Bien!** a television show made in conjunction with Temple TV's production studio. On set, she holds interviews and discussions in a relaxed, open and candid style. With each show, she helps both the featured guest and the audience to confront whatever obstacles they may be facing, and then to bounce back – personally or professionally – despite the intensity or depth of their struggles.

Along with her passion for helping others create positive momentum in their personal development, Lisa has the skill set and experience to assist them in their growth. She holds a Master's degree in Education and has been an adjunct professor at Temple University in Philadelphia for more than 10 years. Lisa teaches business communication at Rowan University in New Jersey.

Her uniquely personal teaching style easily lends itself to either small groups or large crowds. Her core message – *we can all overcome our challenges and love ourselves regardless of what happens to us* – is universal and motivating.

Life happens and will continue to happen. If you are in need of a stimulus for self-transformation, join Lisa Bien, change your perspective, and bounce back.

You can find out more about Lisa on her website: www.LisaBien.com.

38168297R00073

Made in the USA
Middletown, DE
10 March 2019